Alphabet Book

Dominie Press, Inc.

Aa

apple

Bb

boy

Cc

car

Dd

dog

Ee

elephant

Ff

fish

Gg

girl

Hh

horse

Ii

igloo

Jj

jeep

Kk

key

Ll

leaf

Mm

monkey

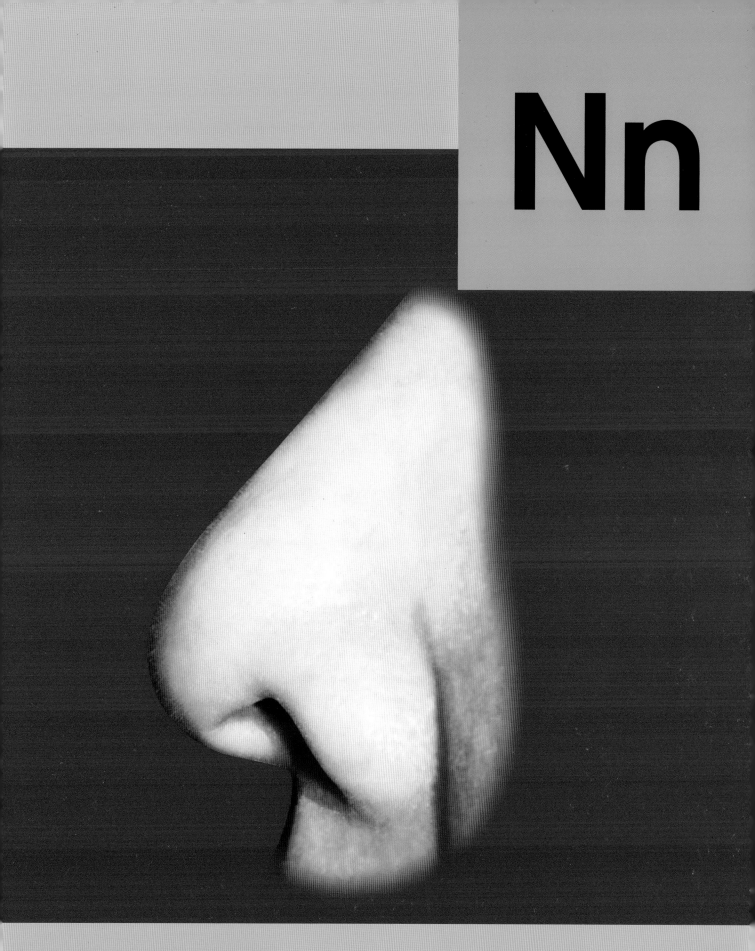

Nn

nose

Oo

octopus

Pp

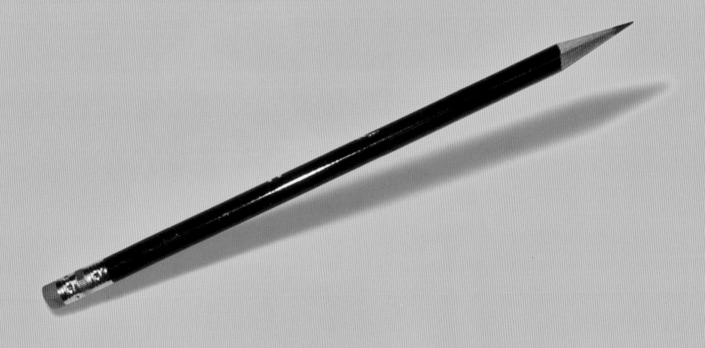

pencil

Qq

queen

Rr

ring

Ss

sun

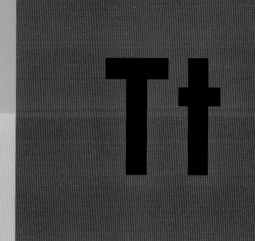

Tt

table

Uu

umbrella

Vv

vest

Ww

watch

Xx

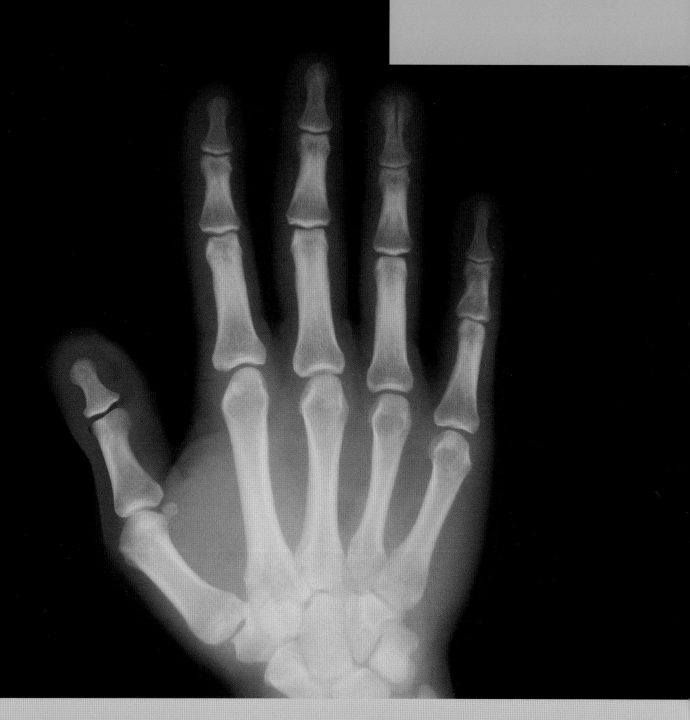

x-ray

Yy

yo-yo

Zz

zebra

Publisher: Christine Yuen
Book Designer: Lois Stanfield
Graphic Designer: Greg DiGenti
Photographs: Graham Meadows (fish), Debra Chew Voss (girl),
    SuperStock (horse, jeep, queen, sun, and x-ray), Corbis (igloo
    and yo-yo), and Kim Westerskov (octopus)

Published by:

⌐ **Dominie Press, Inc.**
1949 Kellogg Avenue
Carlsbad, California 92008 USA
1-800-232-4570
www.dominie.com

Big Book ISBN 0-7685-2984-0
Student Book ISBN 0-7685-2985-9

Printed in Singapore by PH Productions Pte Ltd
1 2 3 4 5 PH 05 04 03